Life in a
17th-Century
Coffee Shop

Life in a
17th-Century
Coffee Shop

THE SUTTON LIFE SERIES

Life in a 17th-Century Coffee Shop

David Brandon

SUTTON PUBLISHING

Sutton Publishing Limited
Phoenix Mill · Thrupp · Stroud
Gloucestershire · GL5 2BU

First published 2007
Copyright © David Brandon, 2007

British Library Cataloguing in Publication Data
A catalogue for this book is available from the British Library.

ISBN 978-0-7509-4639-1

Typeset in Bembo.
Typesetting and origination by
Sutton Publishing Limited.
Printed and bound in England.

Contents

Contents

CHAPTER 1

Introduction

O coffee! Loved and fragrant drink, thou drivest care away . . .

In St Michael's Alley, a narrow, easy-to-miss and quiet passage off Cornhill in the heart of the bustling City of London, stands the Jamaica Wine House. A plaque on the wall explains that on this site stood the original London coffee house, opened in 1652.

Within the coffee houses of the seventeenth and eighteenth centuries a wide range of activities were carried on that had a very important influence on English and international history. The golden age of the coffee house coincided with what can fairly be said to have been an explosion in scientific enquiry and learning. Coffee houses were frequented by such cognoscenti of the arts and sciences as Wren, Dryden, Reynolds, Johnson, Boyle, Swift, Gainsborough, Garrick and Hogarth. The origins of many insurance companies and other businesses in the financial sector can be traced back to men talking to each other in coffee houses. Such was the central role that the coffee houses played in the life of late seventeenth- and eighteenth-century London that gentlemen were often associated more with the coffee houses they frequented than with the homes in which they lived.

Oxford and Cambridge both had coffee houses. Bristol is recorded as having four by 1666, there was at least one at York in 1669 and others in Edinburgh, Glasgow and Dublin. There were also coffee houses in Exeter, Bath, Norwich, Great Yarmouth, Chester, Preston and Warwick. While these were all important provincial towns, given London's unassailable position as the political, economic, social and cultural focus of England, it was inevitable that the majority of coffee houses were to be found there – and it is those in London with which we will mainly be concerned. It is estimated that London, Westminster and their environs had at least 1,000 coffee houses in 1714. In their early days coffee houses were usually identified by a hanging sign, until in 1762 all such signs were banned. A common theme for the sign was either a coffee pot or the turbaned head of a Turk. Common activities of the coffee house, whether in London or elsewhere, were discussion of the news and the conducting of commerce.

Why did coffee-drinking catch on? How did the commodity arrive in Britain? How did the coffee houses operate and what kind of people patronised them? How did they contribute to economic, social and cultural history? Why did they eventually decline? Above all, what was the 'coffee house experience'? What sights, sounds and smells were experienced by those who frequented them? How apt was Dr Johnson's definition of a coffee house as 'A house of entertainment where coffee is sold, and the guests supplied with newspapers'?

This book attempts to get under the skin of the coffee house. It probes the significance of these comparatively fleeting but highly influential institutions and tries to evoke a sense of the historical period of which they were a part and to which they made such a significant contribution. The last decade has seen a remarkable revival in the UK of establishments given over to the adoration and consumption of the roasted coffee bean in drink form. The arrival of this new generation of 'coffee houses' in towns and cities throughout Britain makes it particularly appropriate to go back and take a look at their ancestors.

CHAPTER 2

Early Days

They have in Turkey a drink called coffee made of a berry of the same name, as black as soot, and of a strong scent.

Francis Bacon, 1672

The origins of coffee are confused by a variety of appealing but probably apocryphal legends. The coffee plant bears white, sweet-smelling flowers from which green berries develop. These turn red when ripe. Each berry contains two beans and it is these which are the commercial product of the plant. We know that the coffee plant is almost certainly native to what used to be called Abyssinia, now Ethiopia. There, perhaps accidentally, the locals discovered that the beans of the wild plant, when chewed, helped to sustain their physical and mental spirits during demanding activities in the inhospitable conditions in which they lived and worked. The use of coffee as a drink was first recorded by the revered Arabian philosopher and physician with the Westernised name of Avicenna (980–1037). At that time it seems that the green unroasted beans were simply steeped in boiling water to produce a stimulating and refreshing drink.

The Abyssinians were eventually subjected to raids by Arab slave traders, who picked up the habit of masticating the berries. Finding themselves equally pleased with coffee's stimulant effects, it is likely that these traders rooted up some of the bushes and took them away. It is thought that the coffee plant was first cultivated in the Yemen, probably as a result of the activities of returning slavers.

Legend has it that the real potential of coffee was discovered by an Arab goatherd who was amazed when the animals in his care, in their typically voracious way, not only consumed some of the leaves of a fairly nondescript nearby bush but then started gambolling about in an unusually frisky manner. As the story goes on it sounds even more improbable, with the goatherd telling the imam of the nearby monastery about this experience. It seems that the holy man's main problem was keeping his brethren attentive during long services. Thinking laterally, he picked some of the berries himself, steeped them in water and told his lethargic acolytes to drink the liquid. To his great gratification, he found that they remained rapt in attention and devotion, no matter how tedious and drawn-out their religious offices were.

News spread about the remarkable properties of the fruit of the coffee bush, and the refreshing and stimulating drink was especially appreciated in Muslim countries, where the consumption of alcohol was officially dis-approved of. Apparently two drinks were made from the berry. The first, which we would still recognise today, used roasted and ground berries. This was probably first done in the thirteenth century. The second was a wine made from the fermented skin and the sweetish soft pulp of the berry. This may have been made and consumed surreptitiously.

The consumption of coffee spread throughout the Muslim world in medieval times, and in 1554 seems to have reached Constantinople, which has the first recorded coffee house. So enthusiastically was coffee-drinking adopted there that prayers were neglected. This incurred the wrath of the Muslim authorities, and so the coffee houses were closed. The response of coffee-drinkers was simply to go to each other's houses and enjoy a brew-up there instead.

Francis Bacon (1561–1626), the Tudor polymath, wrote in *Sylva Sylvarum* (published posthumously in 1627):

They have in Turkey a drink called Coffee, made of a berry of the same name, as Black as Soot, and of a strong scent, but not aromatical; which they take beaten in Pouder [*sic*], in Water, as Hot as they can drink it; and they take it and sit at it in the Coffee houses, which are like our Taverns. The drink comforteth the Brain, the Heart, and helpeth digestion.

The consumption of coffee proceeded along trade routes – it was a drink of cosmopolitan people and cosmopolitan places. The first European coffee house was opened in Venice in 1645, and perhaps we should not be surprised to hear that its consumption in the British Isles was first recorded at Oxford in 1637 by a member of Balliol College. A coffee house in Oxford called the Angel was opened in 1652 by a Lebanese, apparently called Jacob. University dons and students found coffee every bit as pleasant and stimulating a drink as had the Muslims. Further coffee houses opened in Oxford.

In the same year, as already mentioned, Pasqua Rosee opened what was probably London's first coffee house, with a sign portraying a Turk's head. He was probably a native of Smyrna, now called Izmir, a port in western Turkey where he had learned how to prepare coffee. He became the servant of a merchant named Daniel Edwards who loved nothing better than socialising and entertaining friends. The strange, even exotic drink that his servant prepared and served up for them was greatly appreciated, not least as a stimulating alternative to alcoholic drinks. Indeed, as its fame spread the bold decision was taken to launch a business selling coffee on premises open to the public.

At first the retailing was done from little more than a stall housed in a shed. The customers stood under an over-hanging awning or in the yard of the nearby St Michael's Church. The business was initially headed up by Pasqua Rosee himself. Rosee, clearly a man with an eye to the promotional value of the media, printed handbills that made extravagant claims for the medicinal properties of coffee. He claimed the drink helped to cure hangovers, and, not content with saying that it also cured dropsy, gout and scurvy, he enlarged on its virtues by explaining that it could prevent miscarriages. According to him, it even facilitated the breaking of wind. Rosee seems to have been something of a rascal: we hear later that he was forced to flee the country and he was last heard of running a coffee house in The Hague.

Hyperbole it may have been that gave coffee its initial impetus in London, but the drink caught on and before Rosee was forced to decamp he moved the business into a house close by. Establishments imitating Rosee's coffee house and its style soon followed. The early ones included Farr's, the Jerusalem, the Jamaica, Garraway's and Jonathan's (both in Change Alley) and Dick's by Temple Bar. Coffee houses quickly became the centre-point of the social life of middle-class London. They owed at least some of their popularity to the fact that the preparation of the coffee involved boiling the water, which of course made the drink safer to consume than water itself.

Coffee was but one of a triumvirate of sober beverages that arrived in Britain within a decade or two of each other, the others being chocolate and tea. All caught on quickly, but coffee and chocolate especially became fashionable and popular. Coffee houses and chocolate houses sprang up like mushrooms in urban centres, and, as with new fashions, they were greeted with both a chorus of praise and mutters of disapproving dissent. The Puritans, whose censorious view of the world dominated England during the Commonwealth, initially approved of the coffee houses because they purveyed non-alcoholic drinks in an atmosphere of respectable sobriety; little could they have foreseen that coffee would go on to become such a widely used drug. Sugar was another colonial product that became important commercially about this time, and it was frequently used in conjunction with the consumption of coffee, chocolate and tea. All these items were evidence of the shrinking nature of the globe.

In a more immediate sense, however, coffee houses were at the centre of the fervid debates that embraced both the tortured last days of the largely unloved Commonwealth and the cases for and against a restoration of the monarchy. These debates gave coffee houses the reputation of being a forum for political debate, much of it subversive and unwelcome, at least in the opinion of those in positions of power. In these heady days of political ferment, republicans toasted their cause with coffee while monarchists saluted the king from over the water with ale and wine.

Among those who used their literary skills to advocate the new phenomena of coffee shops and coffee-drinking was John Aubrey (1626–97). Aubrey's best-known works were his *Miscellanies* (1696) and *Lives* (1693), and although, or perhaps because, he was something of an eccentric, he was well thought of by many of the leading men of letters of the time. He saw coffee houses as places where men could meet and discuss ideas and conduct business in a state of sobriety. He argued that they were therefore a civilising influence, encouraging quiet manners and decorous behaviour. Medical men extolled the virtues of coffee as an alternative to alcohol and its various harmful or unpleasant effects. For some, the attraction of coffee was mainly that it seemed foreign, exotic, vaguely mysterious and somehow sophisticated.

The other side denounced coffee as a black and pernicious drink, and coffee houses as the haunt of idlers, rakes and, even worse, of malcontents bent on spreading political dissent and rebellion. One anti-coffee pamphleteer launched a vituperative attack:

A coffee house is . . . a rota-room that, like Noah's Ark, receives animals of every sort . . . a nursery for training up the smaller fry of virtuosi in confident tattling, or a cabal of kittling critics that have only learnt to spit and mew. . . . It is an exchange where haberdashers of political small-wares meet, and mutually abuse each other and the public with bottomless stories and headless notions; the rendezvous of idle pamphlets and persons more idly employed to read them.

Another observer waxed even more splenetic about the kind of company to be found in coffee houses:

you may see a silly Fop, and a worshipful Justice, a griping Rock, a worthy Lawyer, and an errant Pick-pocket, a reverend Nonconformist and a canting Mountebank; all blended together, to compose an Oglio of Impertinence.

Those who lived and worked close to coffee houses frequently complained of the obnoxious smell that assailed their nostrils when roasting was taking place. In 1657 the proprietor of the Rainbow coffee house in Fleet Street was prosecuted for creating a public nuisance while roasting his beans. Booksellers and others with premises close to coffee houses felt threatened by the fire risk. The keepers of inns, taverns and alehouses were strident in their self-interested criticism of this new form of competition. The craze for coffee-drinking threatened their businesses, since coffee was cheaper. Seeking to make coffee an object of ridicule, even of disgust, they described it as 'syrup and soot' and 'essence of old shoes'.

Such heartfelt outpourings could do little to staunch the burgeoning success that coffee enjoyed in its early days. England was recovering gratefully from the pall of puritanical gloom that had descended on it during the Protectorate of Oliver Cromwell (1653–9). The easy-going atmosphere of the coffee houses struck a chord with the collective mood of the times, and yet these new establishments also provided a more suitable environment for the conducting of business or serious discussion than the frequently raucous and often potentially violent surroundings of many taverns. Some hardened drinkers, however, found coffee houses a great boon: they went to them to cure their hangovers!

The diary of Samuel Pepys, which covers almost ten years, provides a marvellous insight into London middle-class life in the 1660s. To begin with Pepys was an unrepentant devotee of the tavern, but by 1664 visiting the coffee house had established itself as part of his daily routine. He was not overly impressed by the coffee itself but warmed to the convivial socialising that coffee houses encouraged and the wide circle of useful contacts he could make in them. It is evident that for the man about town, whether working for the government, a politician, journalist, literary critic, or simply the man who wanted to feel he was at the centre of things, time spent in the coffee house was time well spent indeed.

It is not widely known that many of the early coffee houses issued their own tokens as substitutes for coins (because of the shortage of small change). The denominations were usually of a halfpenny or farthing, mostly made of brass, copper or pewter, and bore the name of the issuer as well as the value they represented. They could be redeemed at their face value and they were acceptable at all the shops in the neighbourhood of the coffee house concerned.

In 1663 coffee houses had to be licensed. The government was looking for new sources of revenue and it required the proprietors of coffee houses to pay a licence fee of 12*d* as well as a levy of 4*d* per gallon on the coffee they sold. If this was also intended to snuff out their activity in circulating anti-authority political views and information, it did not work. A paradox was that the coffee houses, by virtue of the political discussions that took place in them, provided the opportunity for the government, through its network of agents doubling as patrons, to monitor the state of popular opinion and keep an eye on those they regarded as dangerous subversives.

CHAPTER 3

The Coffee Houses Come of Age

So great a Universitie
I think there ne'er was any
In which you may a scholar be
For spending of a Penny.
'News from the Coffee House', broadside, 1677

Trade in the coffee houses suffered somewhat less than might have been expected during the Plague that ravaged London with such lethal effects in 1665. Casual patrons may have been put off by the Lord Mayor's warning of the danger of 'tippling in taverns, ale houses and coffee houses' as places where contagions might be contracted, but hardbitten devotees of the coffee houses such as Samuel Pepys and Daniel Defoe continued to make their daily visits, taking care however not to chat with strangers. Even those whom they knew well would only be engaged in conversation after polite enquiries had been made about their health and that of the relations they had left back at home. London was of course traumatised by the Plague and the Great Fire that followed it in 1666, but it took remarkably little time for confidence to return and with it the desire to resume the socialising and commercial activity that was associated with the coffee houses. When it did, business boomed.

The rebuilding of the City after the Great Fire started almost immediately. Many coffee houses had been destroyed in the flames, but it was clear that they had already won the hearts of so many Londoners because they were among the first buildings to arise out of the smouldering ruins. Over the fifty years after 1666 large numbers opened their doors for business around the Royal Exchange, Bishopsgate, the Barbican and westwards to Fleet Street, the Strand, Charing Cross, Westminster and St James's, with a smattering south of the Thames in Southwark. The oddest locations for coffee houses were probably that housed in two rooms in the Fleet Prison and that moored on the Thames close to Somerset House.

The remarkable rise in the popularity of coffee houses in London owed something to the capital's spectacular growth in the period from 1650 to 1700. During this time London's population rose from about 375,000 to 490,000, largely as a result of inward migration from the provinces and also from abroad. This meant that London contained large numbers of rootless men for whom the coffee houses offered a welcoming haven and the possibility of making social contacts.

A foreign visitor summed up the attraction of the coffee houses very neatly:

These houses, which are very numerous in London are extremely convenient. You have all Manner of News there. You have a good fire, which you may sit by as long as you please. You have a Dish of Coffee, you meet your Friends for the Transaction of Business, and all for a penny if you don't care to spend more.

Even though coffee houses went on to enjoy their best times over the next fifty years or so, they were never entirely free from criticism. Opposition to coffee house culture came from those women who felt neglected because their husbands were abandoning them for the pleasures of taking coffee and mixing with their like-minded male friends. It is a regrettable but inescapable fact that throughout history men have found a thousand and one excuses when it suited them to enter into the company of their mates. What men did not expect, however, was the opening up of a new and subtle line of attack by the coffee widows. In the pamphlet 'The Women's Petition against Coffee' (1674), it was declared that coffee rendered the men who habitually drank it sterile and even impotent. This raised the spectre of that perennial concern for civil societies, namely a reduction in the birth rate. With tears in their eyes, women explained how men were wilfully turning their backs on their domestic obligations, taking themselves off to enjoy the company of their peers in the coffee houses and threatening the social and economic future of the country by becoming incapable of fulfilling their marital responsibilities – all at the same time. One outspoken critic of coffee alleged that it made men 'as unfruitful as the sandy deserts, from where that unhappy berry is said to be brought'. Some described coffee as 'ninny-broth' and 'Turkey-gruel'.

This was powerful stuff and may have briefly caught men unawares, but they fought back with 'The Men's Answer to the Women's Petition', which boldly vindicated coffee and those who drank it, claiming that 'Coffee collects and settles the Spirits, makes the Erection more Vigorous, the Ejaculation more full, adds a spiritual escency [*sic*] to the Sperme, and renders it more firm and suitable to the Gusto of the Womb, and proportionate to the ardours and expectations too, of the female Paramour.'

Quietly listening to this robust blast and counterblast had been none other than King Charles II himself. He was no friend of the coffee houses, believing them to be nests of sedition where treason was plotted, and he was looking for an excuse to move against them, although he knew that he owed them some kind of debt because within them had taken place at least some of the scheming that had brought about his Restoration. It is often in the interests of those in positions of power to encourage short memories. So it was with Charles. Supporting the female side in the dispute, although definitely no feminist himself, he issued a Royal Proclamation on 29 December 1675 which ordered the closing of all coffee houses within two weeks. Charles of course suffered from the Stuart family delusion that as a monarch he had a divine right to act as an absolutist. The response to his heavy-handed diktat was, however, a demonstration of people power so vehement and determined – in defending coffee houses people were defending freedom of speech – that Charles had little choice but to rescind the proclamation, with the result that he was made to look foolish and the coffee houses remained open. The owners, however, had to give an oath of allegiance to the Crown and undertake not to allow the discussion of subversive or treasonable issues on their premises. This was laughable: such discussion was the very lifeblood of many houses. Predictably, no one took any notice and business went on much as before.

Another source of opposition to the coffee houses had come from the landowning and farming interests who, in 1673, had gone so far as to petition Parliament to prohibit the consumption of tea, coffee and brandy on the grounds that these reduced demand for home-grown produce such as barley, wheat and malt.

In 1681 London endured a prolonged big freeze and the Thames, which was much wider and slower-flowing in those days, was frozen over from December until the following February. The London watermen, temporarily without work but acting as if they owned the river, erected gates at all the water-steps and charged admission. A 'Frost Fair' was held on the ice and a temporary tavern and the Duke's coffee house were erected midstream. This perhaps takes the prize as the most bizarre location for a coffee house. Incidentally, the watermen were noted for their extreme rudeness to their customers and other users of the river, and it was a passing waterman who once espied the distinctive figure of Dr Johnson and rather needlessly called out, 'Sir, under the pretence of keeping a bawdy house, your wife is a receiver of stolen goods!'

An early curiosity among coffee houses was that run by James Salter in Cheyne Walk, Chelsea. It opened in 1695 and gained the name Don Saltero's from one of its regular customers, an admiral who had spent much time cruising off the Spanish coast. Another customer was Sir Hans Sloane (1660–1753), the physician who donated a library of 50,000 volumes and 3,560 manuscripts to form the nucleus of the British Museum. Sloane was a great traveller and had accumulated a large collection of curiosities, some of which he gave to Salter to display in his coffee house. Other patrons deposited items of their own with Salter, which then formed the nucleus of a museum that attracted huge numbers of customers from all over London and elsewhere. Some of the items may have been genuine, such as the sword that had apparently belonged to Oliver Cromwell. Less likely to stand up to scrutiny was 'Pontius Pilate's Wife's Chambermaid's Sister's Hat'. Other items of possibly dubious provenance included a piece of the True Cross, Mary, Queen of Scots' pincushion and a pair of nun's stockings.

The Adam in Shoreditch paid Salter's the compliment of imitation. It exhibited among other items 'teeth that grew in a fish's belly', the comb used by the biblical Abraham on the hair of Isaac and Jacob, Wat Tyler's spurs and the key once used by Adam to lock and unlock the doors to the Garden of Eden.

The English had something of a tradition of consuming hot alcoholic drinks such as possets and punches, some of which were sweet, others spicy. Coffee was unlike anything tried before. Even those who went on to become devotees had to admit that it was an acquired taste – and some never acquired the taste. Its distinctive smell, appearance and flavour and the habits of those who consumed it provided a rich seam for the satirists and wits of the time. According to 'A Satyr against Coffee' (*c.* 1674), coffee was made 'with the scent of old crusts, and shreds of leather burn'd and beaten to powder. It was essence of old shoes, it was horse-pond liquor, witches tipple out of dead men's skulls, it was a foreign fart'.

CHAPTER 4

The Everyday Life of the Coffee House

To limit men's experience, we think not fair,
But let him forfeit twelve-pence that shall swear . . .

P. Greenwood, 'A Brief Description of the Excellent Vertues of
that Sober and Wholesome Drink, called Coffee', 1674

The London coffee house allowed a respectably dressed man, after paying an inclusive admission charge of one penny, to enter well-heated premises furnished not unlike the taverns of the time, where he could smoke a long clay pipe filled with tobacco, provided by the management. He could also sip a dish of coffee or some other beverage, catch up on current affairs either by perusing the newspapers that were available or by listening to or participating in the general discussions that were going on. Equally, he might meet with others to conduct business or simply to socialise. The coffee house was a place of retreat from the company of women who, other than those who worked there in a serving capacity, were not usually allowed entry.

It must be remembered that in the days of the coffee house, drinking was very much a public activity. Coffee houses, beer houses and taverns provided warmth, bustle, conviviality and company – an opportunity for social intercourse in a public forum. To the man about town of those days, especially if he was a bachelor living in what were perhaps not very warm or comfortable lodgings, the coffee house offered a welcoming haven which, in the early days at least, was a respectable home from home to which he could have his letters addressed and at which he could be contacted for much of the time. Servants, for a small financial consideration, would run messages or do errands as required.

Coffee houses became very important places for the circulation of news and other information. The ancestors of today's newspapers appeared in the first half of the seventeenth century, and were often referred to as newsbooks. The ups and downs of the English Civil War of the 1640s stimulated the demand for news, but the authorities, both Parliamentary and Royalist, were suspicious of printed matter, which disseminated information rather than the often salacious tittle-tattle that circulated extensively in broadsides and chapbooks. In 1662, in an attempt to reduce the flow of anti-government and anti-clerical publications, the Printing Act was passed, which meant that all books and pamphlets had to obtain a government licence. In 1665 the *London Gazette* began publishing a mass of official information alongside some news items, but it was turgid stuff and so what can best be described as 'street literature' continued to thrive.

In the 1670s and 1680s a number of unlicensed and therefore illegal papers were produced. The government's power over licensing newspapers lapsed in 1695 and with it the end of official censorship. This led very quickly to the publication of a host of newspapers, many of them tri-weekly, with the first daily, the *Daily Courant*, in 1702. Stamp duty was introduced in 1715 as a handy way of raising tax revenue, while the increased price that resulted would, it was hoped, reduce demand for a communication medium that was often critical of the government and sometimes even subversive. Stamped papers were expensive and the coffee houses played an important role in enabling them to reach a wider audience than their circulation figures might suggest. Inhabited by the 'chattering classes', coffee houses provided an environment in which the contents of the day's papers were read, evaluated and avidly and often loudly discussed, and so became a leading forum in which the discussion of current affairs, the natural sciences, the classics, philosophy and the arts took place. Coffee houses therefore helped to open up access for a much wider range of people to subjects previously reserved for the socially exclusive environment of antiquarian societies, libraries and universities.

The first printed item regularly to contain material other than that of a political nature was possibly the *Athenian Mercury* published early in the second half of the seventeenth century. Much of its content was garnered by men who hung around coffee houses listening to the conversation and, of course, the gossip. A regular feature answered readers' queries – a precursor of the immortal *Brains Trust* programme on BBC radio. Here is a sample:

Is it lawful for a man to beat his wife? Where was the soul of Lazarus for the four days he lay in his grave? What became of the waters after Noah's Flood? Where does extinguished fire go? Why does a horse with a round fundament emit a square excrement?

Items displayed prominently on the walls of coffee houses included advertisements for plays and performances, for auctions and other events. News and ideas interacted. Discussion and debate and the circulation of ideas were the quintessence of the coffee house. They made a significant contribution to the development of the 'information society' of their own and of later ages. The role of coffee houses as places of alternative political debate and activity, however, did little to endear them to the authorities.

Some coffee houses acted as both reference and lending libraries. Many stocked current and back numbers of journals, and, in the case of Peele's, even files of old newspapers. The Chapter, near St Paul's Cathedral, had perhaps the largest collection of books, newspapers and periodicals. The proprietor of one of the first coffee houses to open in Birmingham boasted in 1777 that he could provide all the major London papers, House of Commons division lists, Lloyd's list, all the Irish and most of the country papers and, perhaps curiously, the *Utrecht Gazette*.

The coffee houses played a significant role in the development of the state postal service. Coffee houses were frequently used as accommodation addresses and as receiving and distribution centres for overseas mail, much of which would have arrived in the Pool of London.

Certain standards were expected of those who patronised the coffee houses and sanctions could be applied to those who transgressed the rules. The coffee houses were democratic in the sense that clients were regarded as equal when using the facilities, although the entry fee meant that the establishment was socially exclusive. Audible swearing incurred a financial penalty, quarrelling and discussion of religious matters was disapproved of and even discussions on political issues were expected to be carried out in a seemly fashion. Patrons were required to comport themselves in a cheerful manner, which may have been difficult for those of a naturally saturnine appearance or temperament. Some establishments banned cards and any form of gambling for high stakes. So-called honour was a matter of great importance to the gentlemen of the time and disputes over gambling or even politics or religion must have raised tempers and caused differences of opinion that could only be resolved by one party 'calling out' the other for a duel. This was more likely in the alcohol-charged atmosphere of a tavern than in a coffee house, at least in their early days.

It was in the coffee houses that we can find the origins of the newspaper box-number system. Many people advertised all manner of goods and services through the medium of a box number left at a coffee house. Illicit liaisons could be facilitated by the use of such a system, as could swindles and robberies, which were planned in coffee houses, and the spoils of crimes and scams were divided up there; it was not unknown for the arrest of suspects to take place on their premises.

Another coffee house invention was the ballot box. Sometimes a discussion would generate so much interest and controversy for and against that a vote would be taken. It was felt appropriate that the voting decisions of individuals should be kept secret, and so the ballot box was invented. In coffee house days this was known as 'our wooden oracle', and first appeared at the Turk's Head in Westminster. Tipping also began in the nation's coffee houses. Patrons began to place money in boxes marked 'T.I.P.', short for 'To Insure Promptness' – at least that's how the story goes.

At least one sale of slaves took place in a coffee house, while auctions were common events.

Often a coffee house would have an adjacent room in which auctions and sales could take place, and advertisements for these were posted up in the main public part of the house, known as the coffee room.

All manner of ephemeral material was posted up on the walls and included posters offering rewards to those who could assist in the recovery of stolen property or in some cases runaway servants. In case the patrons could not find enough to discuss concerning the news or the scandals of the day, the walls were often covered with satirical prints, whose purpose was to act as conversation pieces.

The proprietor usually lived on the premises: this is why many had names such as Button's, Will's, Lloyd's and Garraway's. The proprietor frequently acted as an informal host, circulating among the customers, stopping to joke with one here and stopping another there in order to impart the latest piece of juicy gossip – perhaps a 'secret' passed on to him by another customer given to being over-garrulous. He might try to chivvy his customers to take and pay for further refreshment, knowing that he was not going to grow rich on the pennies of those who made one coffee last up to two hours. His wife might preside over the arrangements for preparing the coffee and any other refreshments. The more menial tasks were performed by waiters, male and female, and by serving boys.

Some coffee houses also dispensed sherbet and chocolate, often taken as a substitute for food or a cure for a hangover. Less familiar today was saloop. This was made from the aromatic dried root of the sassafras, a North American laurel. A herbal tea was made from betony, a plant known to present-day gardeners as *Stachys*. The herbal preparations made from this plant had an invigorating effect and if taken in large amounts acted as a purgative and emetic. Also available in coffee houses might be bottled spa water, fruit-flavoured sherbet drinks and lemonade made with freshly squeezed lemons diluted with water and sweetened with sugar or honey. Orangeade followed in due course, and carbonated drinks began to be sold in coffee houses around the end of the eighteenth century.

The first report of tea being available in a coffee house is dated 1658. Tea-drinking was taken up with some enthusiasm by the middle classes in the late seventeenth and eighteenth centuries, but, as we have seen, in the early days tea was extremely expensive and tended to be consumed within the privacy of well-off households. The social rituals surrounding coffee consumption, however, continued to be enjoyed largely in the public surroundings of the coffee house. Thomas Garraway began to offer tea in leaf form on a regular basis from his coffee house in the 1670s, and by 1700 tea had come down somewhat in price and was being sold by grocers and in newfangled teashops. Coffee houses therefore experienced some competition, especially since grocers also started selling coffee in powdered form for home consumption. To counter this threat, many coffee houses began to sell ground coffee in powder form to take away.

An integral part of coffee house culture was the taking of snuff. For those who had to have their nicotine, snuff offered two significant bonuses. It was less antisocial than pipe-smoking, because it created no fumes, and also – and very pertinently, especially in London, aware of the ever-present threat of fire – it did not have to be ignited in order to be enjoyed.

Snuffing first established itself in France, which the English in the eighteenth century rather reluctantly recognised as the most modish, witty and stylish country in Europe. The beau monde of London, Edinburgh, Bath and elsewhere during the period known as the Enlightenment rushed eagerly to absorb France's philosophy, literature, manners and therefore its habit of sniffing rather than smoking tobacco.

The onward march of snuff was undoubtedly promoted by the fact that no fewer than 50 tons of it were captured by a naval force under the command of Admiral Sir George Rooke from a combined French and Spanish fleet at the Battle of Vigo in 1702. The use of snuff then became valued in England as a trophy of the Royal Navy's victory in battle. Snuffing is now almost extinct in Britain and it is often regarded as a curious and somewhat repulsive habit. The snuff is inhaled with the intention of provoking a sneeze. If a sneeze is achieved, the pleasure gained is thought of as being almost equal to that of an orgasm. While this may obviously help to explain the popularity of snuff-taking in the eighteenth century, it has to be said that the pleasure of the good old orgasm has proved more enduring.

The user of snuff would take a pinch of the tobacco dust between thumb and forefinger, hold it against one nostril and then the other and sniff sharply. He would have a handkerchief or his sleeve at the ready and would hope that these would catch whatever was explosively discharged from his nostrils. This might work. When it did not, those close by were showered with a fine spray composed of a mixture of tobacco grains together with a rich variety of microscopic disease-bearing organisms.

Dr Johnson was a devotee both of snuff and of coffee house culture. In 1773 he commented, 'Smoking has gone out. To be sure, it is a shocking thing, blowing smoke out of our mouths into other people's mouths, eyes and noses, and having the same done to us.' This rotund and vivacious if somewhat irascible man was himself a devotee, even a slave, of snuff, which he took in vast quantities, expelling it copiously into the atmosphere around him and liberally anointing both those people in his immediate neighbourhood and his own clothes.

It could be an important financial coup for a coffee house if it became indelibly associated in people's minds with being the haunt of a particular celebrity. In the early days Will's was such a place, where people would expect to find the poet John Dryden, while Joseph Addison the essayist and politician was associated particularly with Button's. Several generations later, Thomas Telford

(1757–1834), the eminent Scottish civil engineer, made the Salopian his base. A companionable man, Telford had a wide circle of friends and acolytes, and his presence brought so much trade that when the business was sold he was mentioned as being one of the assets and a major selling point.

A feature of coffee houses in their early days was the presence on the premises of quacks, who plied their business there. In 1710 one Thomas Smith, styling himself 'first master Corn-Cutter of England', daily worked his way around twenty-one coffee houses in London attending to those suffering with this painful affliction. Quacks would attempt to ingratiate themselves with the proprietor or preferably his wife and try to arrange for their nostrums to be on display and even available for purchase close to the entrance. As Addison noted in the *Tatler* (19–21 October 1721), 'The walls of the coffee houses were hung round with gilt frames containing the bills of "Golden Elexirs", "Popular Pills", "Beautifying Waters", "Drops and Lozenges", all as infallible as the Pope.'

The best advertisement a quack could wish for was to be noticed. One by the name of Van Butchell rode around the streets of the City mounted on a small white horse on which he had painted purple spots. He gave out handbills promoting his products and then made his way to his favourite coffee house to see whether his efforts had attracted any new customers. Obviously the proprietor was happy with this arrangement because those who turned up to buy the quack's products would probably also be persuaded to stay for refreshment.

Few quacks made such bold claims for their skills as an Italian called Lattese, who was based at the Antigallican near the Royal Exchange. Lattese claimed to have discovered a method whereby aspiring parents could predetermine the sex of their unborn child. Needless to say, his service came with a hefty price tag, but it is likely that he had plenty of takers. A quack named Stringer visited the City coffee houses peddling an elixir he claimed would restore youthful health, vigour and looks. Modestly he added that it also cured the gout.

In the eighteenth century many of the coffee houses' customers would have arrived by sedan chair, the taxi-cab of the time. The sedan had one advantage over all modern conveyances: it offered total protection from the rain. If the customer wished, the sedan was brought right into his hall. Nor was there any need to brave the elements at the other end, because the chair could be carried directly into the hall of the coffee house itself. The early sedans were heavy and cumbersome but lighter ones appeared in the 1770s. They tended to be used mainly by women. Men users were thought of as sissies and had to run the gauntlet of catcalls – the one intended to cause the most hurt being 'Frenchie!'

The chairmen were generally notorious for their grumpiness and their lack of what would now be called 'customer care'. Carrying a sedan containing a portly gentleman for distances of perhaps a mile or more over cobblestones and setts made slippery by rain or ice could not, however, have been an easy matter. It is interesting that other men providing public transport also had a reputation for rudeness. They included, particularly notoriously, the Thames watermen but also omnibus conductors, otherwise known as 'cads', and the early drivers of hansom cabs.

CHAPTER 5

Coffee House Sights, Sounds and Smells

the coffee house is the sanctuary of health, the nursery of temperance, the delight of frugality, academy of civility, and free-school of ingenuity.

The man passing along a street in the City of London or in Westminster knew when there was a coffee house close by. His eyes might light on the hanging sign – he might even be hit by it if he was on horseback and the sign was swinging wildly in the wind. Either way, his nostrils were likely to be assailed by the aroma of roasting coffee. If it was night-time, the entrance would probably be brightly lit.

Nothing else was quite like the atmosphere of the coffee house. A penny was paid at the door, entitling the visitor to all the services available but also as a tacit recognition that he was prepared to observe the rules of the house. A penny was good value for money but enough to deter the poorer elements of society, as was the intention.

In 'The London Spy' (1709) Ned Ward, an acute, if slightly world-weary, observer gives us a flavour of what to expect upon entering a coffee house:

> In we went, where a packet of muddling muckworms were busy as so many rats in an old cheese-loft, some going, some coming, some scribbling, some talking, some drinking . . . and the whole room stinking of tobacco like a Dutch barge or a boatswain's cabin.

We could expect there to be a babble of voices and for the atmosphere to be thick and slightly opaque as almost tangible clouds of acrid tobacco smoke wafted to and fro. The draughts set up by the opening and closing of doors added another element to this heady brew as puffs of smoke from the fire of sea coal billowed out to add their own distinctive contribution to the fug. Another sensuous element within was the aroma given off as coffee was roasted and brewed, a continuous process on busy days.

The human occupants of the coffee house contributed another component to this olfactory cornucopia. The men of yesteryear considered it either effeminate or actually downright harmful to wash, let alone bathe. Those who liked to think of themselves as fashionable men about town, the fops of the day (sometimes referred to as macaronis), doused themselves in scent, thereby creating what would seem to us a particularly malodorous mixture when it was combined with the smells of their various bodily emanations. Added to this would be the aroma given off by the perfumed pomades with which most men anointed their hair.

The seventeenth, eighteenth and nineteenth centuries – the age of the coffee house – were the days when gentlemen travelled either on horseback or in horse-drawn conveyances. The streets were reeking morasses of mud and filth in wet weather, and dust bowls in dry periods. Much of the ordure consisted of horse droppings. This mixed seamlessly with the mud and other dirt such as household refuse and human excrement that covered the streets and the so-called pavements. It was simply impossible to move around the streets without accumulating quantities of this nastiness on one's clothes. When the weather was dry, a carriage passing swiftly down the street or a sudden gust of wind would stir up a cloud of dusty filth which got into the eyes, the nose and the mouth and settled in the hair and on clothing. Dirt also came down chimneys and through open and even closed doors and windows. It was everywhere. The heat generated by the fires and the close-packed humanity caused the occupants to sweat profusely. Small streams of perspiration would carve runnels through the patina of filth overlying people's visages.

In cold weather the first arrivals would cluster around the fireplace, warming their backsides and showing scant concern for latecomers entering from the freezing streets. The more extravert would start holding forth to the coteries who gathered around them. As the day wore on, and if business was brisk, new arrivals would have little option but to jostle and elbow their way through a seething mass of close-packed male humanity in order to find those whom they wanted to socialise with or had arranged to meet on professional and other matters. Others of more solitary disposition might head for the latest broadsheets and newspapers, if these hadn't already been monopolised or removed by earlier visitors.

The coffee house's celebrities held court. Each one had a favourite corner, an unmarked but reserved spot, and their disciples and assorted sycophants and toadies would try to huddle as close as possible while hanging on to every utterance made by the great master. Noise levels rose as more patrons squeezed in. While it was not regarded as acceptable to raise one's voice in anger, the general hubbub meant that people had little option but to speak ever louder if conversation and listening were to be sustained. It should not be thought that the discourses were always on weighty subjects: gossip and scandalmongering were well to the fore and many were the reputations that were made or broken in the capital's coffee houses.

Coffee houses were what we would now call a 'poseur's paradise'. Egos swelled as their owners held forth to anyone within earshot on any manner of subject about which they happened to have a smattering of knowledge. Ignorance was no obstacle to declamations on other topics about which they knew absolutely nothing. As ever, the loudest noise was often made by those with the least useful contribution to make. Some especially pretentious characters carried out their conversations in Latin or hailed the servants in Greek when they wanted more coffee. Others would strut around like popinjays showing off their latest finery. Pepys recorded the occasion on which he first wore his 'best black cloth suit, trimmed with scarlet ribbon, very neat'.

Almost everyone smoked and the normal procedure was to pick up a clay pipe on entering the premises. As the day wore on and it began to get dark outside, it also became gloomier inside. The oil lamps and candles would be lit but would fight an often unequal battle with the smog and the generally thickening atmosphere. It might become too dark to read. The fug which pervaded every corner of the coffee house elicited the scorn of at least one writer:

The room stinks of tobacco worse than Hell of Brimstone, and is as full of Smoak as their heads that frequent it, whose humours are as various as those of Bedlam, and their discourse of times as heathenish and dull as their liquor. (From 'The Character of a Coffee-House with the Symptomes of a Town-wit' (1673).)

A bar would take up one end or a corner of the coffee room, but the dominating feature was likely to be one or more long wooden tables. These tables would be littered with newspapers, broadsheets and all sorts of other printed matter. The patrons would perch on long benches around the tables, which might be equipped with pens and other writing materials. As 'coffee house culture' developed over the years, other tables would appear at which smaller groups of patrons could conduct their business or simply chew the fat. The communal nature of the coffee house was further eroded when booths with high backs made their appearance. These allowed the inmates more privacy in which to conduct their affairs.

The coffee that was dispensed in these establishments bore little resemblance to that consumed in the twenty-first century. It was brewed in great pots containing between 8 and 10 gallons of liquid and was served piping hot without milk or cream. It is likely that coffee house customers found straight coffee too bitter and that before long they began to add milk and sugar to taste. Various other ingredients were added to the brew, the resulting concoctions sounding strange to our ears. These included ale or wine, and herbs and spices such as cloves, cinnamon or spearmint. Patrons had to pay more for these exotic brews, some of which would have exuded a bouquet that gave yet another dimension to the already rich cocktail of smells that assailed the nostrils of those who had just entered the room.

In one corner stood a large fire and grate which supported a boiler, a device on which the beans were roasted and the cups, bowls and other vessels kept warm. The coffee mill was invented in 1687 and greatly improved the quality of the product. Cupboards, often with glass fronts, displayed spare drinking vessels, scales and weights, candlesticks, candles and other necessities. The owner was likely to be presiding over this activity. It might even be a woman.

Tobacco smoking enjoyed enormous popularity throughout the age of the coffee house and was an integral part of coffee house culture. The clay pipes patrons picked up on entering the premises were cheap and disposable. Their shape changed over the years with the stem becoming progressively longer, evolving in the early 1800s into the 'churchwarden' or 'yard of clay' pipe. It needed but few patrons to be sucking and drawing on these pipes for the room to become full of a pungent, semi-opaque and choking nimbus of tobacco fumes. This atmosphere was by no means to everyone's liking: a French visitor in 1729 described his first impression of London's coffee houses in disparaging terms. According to him they were 'not over clean or well-furnished, owing to the quantity of people who resort to these places and because of the smoke which would quickly destroy good furniture'.

The hubbub of the coffee house would be punctuated at frequent intervals by the loud sneezes that accompanied snuff-taking. These sneezes, if not trapped by handkerchief or sleeve, sent a fine, scarcely perceptible spray of droplets into the atmosphere that were inevitably inhaled by all around including, of course, those who had no wish to partake of snuff or other people's germs and who loathed the snuff-taking habit. Various substances were mixed with snuff. Some were simply cheap additives designed to increase the blenders' profit margins. Others were aromatic with an effect not unlike perfume. These added yet another ingredient to the heady bouquet of the coffee house.

Regular customers had their own distinctive snuff-boxes, which were kept on shelves and handed down to them as they entered. The snuffbox belonging to John Dryden was proudly displayed at Will's coffee house long after he had died. He had held court there regularly for many years and his presence had attracted a great deal of business. The opening and shutting of snuffbox lids was a constant element among the myriad auditory sensations apparent in a busy coffee house. As the satirist Ned Ward put it, 'the clashing of the snuff-box lids, in opening and shutting, made more noise than their tongues; and sounded as terrible in my ears as the melancholy tick of so many death-watch beetles.'

However, the clack of snuffboxes was only one element in the sheer racket that marked the everyday business of the coffee house. The cacophony also included a background of conversation varying in cadence and volume with the vehemence of the participants – the slurp of coffee being sipped, kettles, cups, pots and bowls rattling, the scraping of chairs and banging of doors, the splutter as customers cleared their throats and sometimes expectorated. It is a wonder that those who made their way to coffee houses to conduct serious business ever managed to get anything done. It is clear that coffee houses in their glory days were the places where London's 'movers and shakers' conducted much of their business, be it commercial, political, cultural, intellectual or recreational, in what they considered to be a congenial atmosphere and surroundings.

CHAPTER 6

A Coffee House for Every Cause and Interest

All nations use coffee as an aid to conversation.

P.G. Hamerton, The Intellectual Life

One of the most obvious characteristics of the coffee houses was how each tended to attract a specialised clientele. They became the acknowledged meeting place for members of a particular profession or occupation, for those with shared aims – perhaps what would now be called an interest group – or sometimes simply for those who wanted the company of the like-minded.

Often the kind of clientele who used a particular coffee house reflected the activities that were carried on in that part of London. Lloyd's and Garraway's, for example, attracted the businessmen in the financial quarter around the Royal Exchange in the City of London. In Westminster

St James's and the Cocoa-Tree were much used by politicians, the former associated with the Tories, the latter with the Whigs. Many coffee houses were sited close to St Paul's Cathedral and frequented by clergymen and intellectuals eager to debate theological and philosophical issues.

Will's Coffee House in Covent Garden, once a seedy drinking den called the Red Cow, was famed as the resort of London's literati. The self-appointed guru of Will's was the poet and playwright John Dryden (1631–1700). Here he held forth to a rapt audience with his views on the most recently published or performed poems and plays, and his reputation was such that many highly distinguished men of letters such as Samuel Pepys and Alexander Pope became habitués of Will's, eager to absorb his latest pronouncements. This probably gave Dryden undue power as a literary critic and an arbiter of literary taste. Unimpressed by Will's was the acerbic Irish clergyman and wit Jonathan Swift, who in 'Hints to an Essay on Conversation' disparagingly wrote of the company he observed there:

The worst conversation I ever remember to have heard in my life was that at Will's Coffeehouse, where the wits (as they were called) used formerly to assemble; that is to say,

five or six men who had writ plays . . . entertained one
another with their trifling composures in so important an
air, as if they had been the noblest efforts of human
nature, or that the fate of kingdoms depended on them.

On Dryden's death, Will's rapidly changed its character
and became devoted to the gambling craze of the time. Its
mantle was later assumed, among others, by Button's Coffee
House, also in Covent Garden. Here the guiding light was
Joseph Addison (1672–1719), essayist and politician.
Addison contributed to the *Tatler* magazine started by his
close friend Richard Steele in 1709 and to its more
significant successor, the *Spectator*. The *Tatler* mainly
concerned itself with literature, manners and morals, and
advocated moderation and toleration in politics and
religion. The *Spectator* had a wide and prestigious readership
and Will's, Addison and Steele between them were
unquestionably highly influential in spreading the idea of a
liberal 'polite' culture among the educated middle classes of
the time. As Dr Johnson said in his *Life of Addison*, Addison
and his coterie 'had a perceptible influence on the conversation of the time, and taught the frolic and the gay to unite
merriment with decency'.

The Grecian Coffee House gained a reputation for being a rendezvous for those of an intellectual bent. In 1709 the *Tatler* recorded that many of its patrons were classical scholars who 'generally spent the evening . . . in enquiries into antiquity, and thought anything news which gave . . . new knowledge'. Their esoteric activities included attempting to arrange the events in the *Iliad* and the *Odyssey* in chronological order. To us, this seems a harmless if perhaps a trifle pointless exercise and it seems strange that on one occasion the emotions aroused by it were sufficient to cause two patrons to sort out their differences with swords, the outcome being that one of the antagonists stabbed the other to death.

Individual coffee houses might go out of fashion. This happened to Button's after the death of Addison and Steele, an establishment whose role passed to the Bedford Coffee House in Covent Garden. The Bedford's list of devotees was a glittering one. It included the half-brothers John (1721–80) and Henry Fielding (1707–54). The former, blind from birth, was a pioneer of policing and a magistrate who was often referred to as 'the Blind Beak'. The latter was a prolific writer. His major work, *The History of Tom Jones, a Foundling*, is regarded as one of the earliest and most influential English novels. In the Bedford they hobnobbed, *inter alia*, with William Hogarth (1697–1764), the artist and engraver, Oliver Goldsmith (1728–74), playwright, novelist and poet, and David Garrick (1717–79), the eminent actor, playwright and theatre manager. How such men must have revelled in the intellectual badinage, the sparkling repartee and the cut-and-thrust as barbed verbal witticisms were exchanged, with no quarter expected or given!

A perhaps less Bohemian clientele flocked to the Grecian Coffee House in Devereaux Court off the Strand. Many of these were Fellows of the Royal Society such as the scientist Sir Isaac Newton (1642–1727), Edmund Halley (1656–1742), the eminent astronomer, and Sir Hans Sloane (1660–1753), who, as we have seen, was a physician and avid collector of scientific items and also of books and manuscripts.

Politics was the staple item of news and discussion in the coffee houses located in the Westminster district. Whigs and Tories made sure they patronised different establishments. For the best part of a century, these clubs witnessed the comings and goings of many of the country's leading statesmen, rank-and-file MPs, a covey of sycophants, placemen, gossip columnists, scandalmongers and general men about town. Most of these coffee houses eventually metamorphosed into exclusive gentlemen's clubs.

Jonathan's Coffee House in Exchange Alley was opened for business about 1680 and soon gained the reputation of being a meeting place for political subversives. Later on the place became associated with what might be called financial subversion, as the place where many of the dubious deals were made that, taken together, constituted the South Sea Bubble of 1719–20. This, Britain's greatest-ever speculative boom, a heady mix of get-rich-quick greed and gullibility, inevitably collapsed, with many prominent people losing heavily, some even committing suicide, and the City of London's reputation for financial probity seriously damaged.

In 1745 there was widespread alarm in London about Bonnie Prince Charlie, the Young Pretender, marching down from Scotland and gathering an army to throw King George II off the throne. The louche characters who continued to frequent Jonathan's saw this as a window of opportunity and persuaded many to part with large sums of money by speculating on whether or not the rebellion would be successful. From 1762 until 1773 Jonathan's in effect came to act as the City's first stock exchange.

One of London's most famous insurance institutions traces its ancestry directly back to the coffee houses. Edward Lloyd owned a coffee house at 16 Lombard Street in the City of London. From around 1700 auctions of ships and of cargoes were held there, and so the coffee house attracted many customers involved in marine underwriting. In the congenial and informal atmosphere of Lloyd's, men of like interests met and it was but a short step for them to start conducting much of their business in the coffee house rather than on the floor of the Royal Exchange. By 1727 the business of underwriting ships and cargoes was formally moved to Lloyd's and remained there until 1771. In that year Lloyd's of London was set up, formally bringing together the shipping underwriters who used to frequent the coffee house.

As London grew into the world's major banking and insurance centre, Britain was reaching its economic and industrial ascendancy as 'the workshop of the world'. In parallel with this, Lloyd's and other coffee houses, from serving as makeshift places of work where business was combined with pleasure, became the nuclei around which the financial institutions of the City of London developed. Little use was made of offices in the modern sense.

Merchants, brokers, bankers and miscellaneous traders lived in or close to the City and tended to do their business in the Royal Exchange or the taverns and coffee houses clustered in large numbers nearby. Important overseas trading concerns such as the East India Company and the Hudson's Bay Company all made considerable use of the coffee houses, as did the City Livery Companies, both for formal meetings and for social purposes.

The patrons of Bastons in Cornhill were largely medical men who used the place not only to discuss professional developments with each other but to provide consultations with their patients who knew that this was a place where they could find them. The eighteenth-century equivalent of estate agents went to the London on Ludgate Hill, while the George in the Strand drew its clientele from the legal profession. Booksellers flocked to the Chapter, in Paternoster Row, itself the centre of the bookselling trade.

The fashionable young men about town, the bucks and the beaux, repaired to Man's in Scotland Yard. Some of them had little ready cash but were desperate to keep up appearances, to see and be seen while spending as little as possible. Coffee houses suited them ideally because the small entry charge allowed them to show off their finery and to while away two or three hours over one bowl of coffee while surrounded by their fellows and feeling that they were at the centre of haute couture.

Tom's, close to the Strand, enjoyed an eclectic clientele. At one time the proprietor was Thomas Twining, and the coffee house communicated through a narrow passage with his shop, where tea and coffee were sold. One of its patrons was Christopher Wren, son of the illustrious architect and astronomer. He did not match his father's achievements but, like every dog, he had his day. This was when, in 1710, in the presence of his father, he laid the last stone of the lantern that tops the dome of St Paul's Cathedral. Another regular was Edmund Curll, notorious as a publisher of scatological literature from whose name the eponym 'Curlicism' was derived. More staid customers included visiting country clergymen and attorneys from provincial towns.

The Chapter Coffee House in Paternoster Row close to St Paul's Cathedral was patronised by the tragic Thomas Chatterton (1752–70). Born and brought up in Bristol, Chatterton began to write verse while he was still at school. At the age of 14 he was apprenticed to an attorney, employment which he loathed, and probably from boredom and frustration published a piece of pseudo-archaic prose in a Bristol periodical, claiming to have found the original in a forgotten chest in a local church. Since this attracted the interest of local antiquarians, Chatterton then provided a host of other skilfully produced forged documents. Among these were works by an imaginary fifteenth-century Bristol monk and poet called Thomas Rowley. The documents aroused great interest, and although some critics doubted the authenticity of the material, others championed the new finds. Bathing in the limelight, Chatterton moved to London. On the death of his patron, for whom he produced a stream of further forgeries, his publishers abandoned him because of growing doubts about whether the items were genuine. Penniless and lonely, living in a miserable garret, Chatterton took his own life. Debates about the authenticity of his output continued for many years, a number of critics acclaiming the merit of his work even if its provenance was not as he claimed. His work stirred literary figures of the calibre of Wordsworth who described him as 'The marvellous Boy, The sleepless Soul that perished in his pride', while Keats described him as 'the purest writer in the English language'.

CHAPTER 7

The Decline of the Coffee House

We rightly speak of a storm in a teacup as the tiniest disturbance in the world, but out of a coffee-cup come hurricanes.

R.W. Lynd, The Blue Lion, c. 1930

Chapter 6 explained how some of the coffee houses of the City of London, from simply being places where the pursuit of business and pleasure were combined in congenial surroundings, went on to play a crucial role in developing the culture that led the City to dominate the world's financial markets for several generations. Other coffee houses attracted politicians, while others still were patronised by eggheads and highbrow thinkers.

However, not all London's coffee houses were devoted to the conduct of business, the shenanigans of politics or the sharpening of the intellect. England's Augustan days, which witnessed a flowering of achievement in the arts and sciences and coincided with the heyday of the coffee houses, were also a time of unashamedly raffish and frequently robust hedonism. There were plenty of coffee houses that functioned as the gathering places of rakehells, card-sharpers, scoundrels of every kind and those who were well-to-do but dissipated. The activities that took place in these haunts cast a shadow over the rest and probably contributed to the decline of coffee houses.

Among those who had cash to spare and not infrequently among those who did not, gambling reached almost epidemic proportions in the eighteenth century, and certain coffee houses provided the surroundings in which hours were passed playing cards or other games of chance. Almost anything served as an excuse for a bet. Men backed their fancies on the racecourse and the cricket field; they laid wagers on the size of the bag after a day's shooting, on the outcomes of boxing matches, cockfights and bouts of bear-baiting; they bet on whether or not a fox would escape the hunt, on the speed at which a new cabriolet could be driven, on how soon a friend's affair with the housemaid would end and the probability that a child would or would not be produced by the illicit liaison – and, if it was, which sex it would be. They even staked small fortunes on which of two drips running down a pane of glass would reach the bottom first!

The doubts regarding the sex of the Chevalier d'Eon de Beaumont (1728–1810) provoked a flurry of wagering in the 1770s. He had arrived in London in 1762 as an embassy official. Beaumont was in fact a French lawyer and ex-dragoon, one of the finest swordsmen in France and a natty cross-dresser, totally convincing wherever he went in whichever gender role he was performing. Those who thought he was female pointed to his apparent total lack of amorous interest in women. His sex and the nature of his sexuality remained a source of salacious speculation for two decades or more. He turned up one day at Garraway's having heard that sums of 100 guineas or more were being staked on his sex. He challenged any man to disprove that he was a male by fighting a duel with him. His reputation had preceded him and there were no takers. A post-mortem revealed that he was indeed a man. Many fortunes were won and lost that day!

Of those places to which the gambling fraternity was attracted, White's Chocolate House was probably the best known. This was founded in 1693 by an anglicised Italian,

Francis White, in St James's Street, close to Westminster. It is unlikely that it ever served cocoa. White's features in the sixth print of William Hogarth's moralistic visual saga *A Rake's Progress*, published in 1735. Despite inheriting a small fortune from his father, a miserly usurer, Tom Rakewell is a feckless youth apparently bent on self-destruction. His money provides him with a lavish and fashionable lifestyle but he is ill at ease with fine society and is drawn to the raunchy delights offered by the brothels of Covent Garden. Rakewell is robbed, and it is not long before he is arrested for debt. Desperate to escape insolvency, he marries a toothless, gnarled crone, aged but rich. His headlong plunge into perdition continues as he quickly sets about spending his newly acquired wealth. In *Scene in a Gaming House*, Rakewell is portrayed in White's plunged into fury and despair having just lost everything at the gaming table. Hogarth was not afraid to name names, and among the others shown in the debauched scene he portrays is Lord William Manners, a brother of the Duke of Rutland. Unlike many others, Manners made a fortune as a professional gambler and by doing so incurred the judgemental Hogarth's severe disapproval. Rakewell for his part ends up in Bethlehem

Hospital, the notorious 'Bedlam' which housed the incurably insane. Fire destroyed White's in 1773, but it reopened some time later as White's Club, possibly the first of many London coffee houses to become a private club.

By this time many coffee houses had become places of ill repute. They were the resort of disreputable rakes, card-sharpers, confidence tricksters and quacks surreptitiously peddling all manner of worthless nostrums and panaceas. Highwaymen were sometimes customers, patiently sitting, watching and listening, thereby getting a good idea of who was likely to be leaving the premises with enough money or other items to make them worth robbing. Spies lurked in corners, hoping to pick up titbits of intelligence about the customers' political views, which they would then eagerly relay to their paymasters. False witnesses and mischief-makers used coffee houses to spread scurrilous and damaging rumours such as that of the Popish Plot, a sinister scheme to overthrow the political system in England and restore Roman Catholicism to its former pre-eminence. For places dominated by men, who were supposed to be above such things, a good deal of mere gossip and tittle-tattle went on in the coffee houses.

Some coffee houses became little more than fronts for brothels, or at least trysting places for illicit liaisons, and locations in which members of both sexes solicited for sexual favours. Most such establishments advertised the services they offered by painted signs outside, the significance of which would have been immediately evident to those men out on the town and looking for a good time. The sign of the star outside a coffee house was a clear indication of the pleasures on offer within. Another sign with the same purpose depicted a woman's arm or hand holding a coffee-pot. These establishments were described by a foreign observer as 'temples of Venus'. It was by no means unknown for coffee houses to be owned by women who had made enough money from prostitution, usually of the rather superior sort, to go into semi-retirement in the coffee house business. Their professional experience might then come in handy. Two such women were Moll King and Anne Rochford.

Moll was the owner of King's Coffee House in Covent Garden. This had unusually liberal opening hours, ostensibly to serve the needs of market-workers with whom it was popular as it was also with men and women in pursuit of sexual pleasure. King's was little more than a brothel, but Moll escaped prosecution because she took care to ensure that there were no beds on the premises. Like Moll, Anne featured as the main character in a highly obscene and largely fictional biography and ran a coffee house of dubious propriety. She herself, at least while in her prime, had been a woman of considerable beauty, nicknamed by some 'the Pineapple of Great Britain' because she possessed the flavours of all the world's delicious fruits.

The rules that had been posted up for all to see in the coffee houses, the observation of which made them accepted as meeting places for 'respectable' gentlemen, gradually fell into disuse. Coffee was seen as a stimulant, contrasting with alcohol, which often led its users first of all to be simply silly and then later on unpleasantly argumentative. In the early days, strong drink was served in only a few coffee houses, but a significant part in the coffee house's fall from grace was played by alcoholic drinks, particularly wine, which many of them later started to serve. Inevitably this sometimes changed the nature of the discussions and lively, even impassioned, arguments that were the life blood of the coffee houses. From being sparkling and witty, they easily degenerated into drunken, angry exchanges that could lead to fights or even duels. In the 1770s a French army officer drinking in St James's was stabbed by another patron apparently because he would not take the conversation seriously and insisted on laughing. The previously decorous atmosphere of the coffee house was to be irreparably damaged by the introduction of alcohol.

Curiously enough, the insidious spread of alcohol into the coffee houses took place at a time when there was a powerful move to regulate manners and public behaviour. Social intercourse was an increasingly public activity, taking place in coffee houses, taverns, pleasure gardens, the various facilities specifically designed for the purpose in the larger and more modish spas, in assembly rooms and in theatres. Accepted codes of conduct were a necessary part of the good manners and decorum required of polite society. Jonathan Swift defined good manners as: 'the art of making people easy with whom we converse'. Such unwritten rules were applied primarily to the upper and upper middle classes and acted as bonding agents, but it was hoped that their observance would filter down to the lower orders, which were seen as increasingly truculent and disrespectful. So far as coffee houses were concerned, the tenor of the social, political and business discussions that took place there would depend on the observation of simple common-sense rules concerning sobriety, moderation, the acceptance of different opinions and mutual respect and politeness. As we have seen, this worthy objective was only partly achieved, but the insidious spread of alcohol into the coffee houses, often accompanied by gambling rather than polite conversation and good fellowship, brought about the beginning of the long decline of coffee house culture.

Some coffee houses took up the sale of alcoholic drinks with such enthusiasm that they virtually became taverns where coffee was also sold. In 1731 one such establishment opened its doors in Ludgate Hill going by the ponderous name of the London Coffee House, Punch-House, Dorchester Beer and Welsh Ale Warehouse.

It was perhaps inevitable that the disreputable character assumed by a minority of coffee houses tended to stigmatise the rest and contributed to their decline. Those at the top end of the social scale, worried that they might lose their largely exclusive clientele, transformed themselves into expensive members-only clubs. One of the first to do so started as a gentlemen's club meeting in Tom's in Russell Street, with many eminent members including Dr Johnson, David Garrick and Sir John Fielding. This kind of development undoubtedly contributed to the protracted decline of the coffee house.

The gentlemen's clubs of London unquestionably have their origins in the coffee houses of Augustan London. As certain coffee houses became associated with those supporting particular causes, activities or interests, a room within the premises would be hired for their meetings. If they progressed and eventually formed a members' club, especially one that prospered with wealthy and influential clients, it was just a simple and logical step to put in an offer that the proprietor could probably not refuse whereby the club bought the premises for their own exclusive use. Perhaps the former proprietor would be kept on as manager.

The gentlemen's clubs retained but improved on many of the facilities of the coffee house. They turned their back on the principle of openness to all, although in reality large sections of the poorer population had always been effectively excluded from coffee houses. They offered high-quality cuisine in luxurious surroundings, alcoholic and other refreshment, overnight accommodation, gaming facilities, writing materials, a supply of newspapers and periodicals and best of all as far as the members were concerned, a sense of exclusivity.

An example of the way in which a coffee house metamorphosed seamlessly into a gentlemen's club was White's. Founded as we have seen in 1693, the business was initially known as White's Chocolate House and always aspired to serving the upper end of the market, levying an entry charge of twopence. It soon developed a reputation as the place where rather dissipated aristocrats gambled for high stakes and often lost. White's underwent a number of vicissitudes, but in 1736 was clearly moving in the direction of becoming a private club. In that year part of the premises became an inner club, with entry restricted to members who had been elected by ballot. In 1781 White's became a members-only private club.

Men who had serious business to conduct increasingly decided that it could be done more conveniently without the various diversions offered by the coffee houses. The hard negotiations might be done in offices or elsewhere in private and only then would some socialising take place in a tavern or nearby coffee house.

By the end of the eighteenth century, coffee was coming down in price but it was experiencing growing competition from tea, which had previously been much more expensive. Tea was usually consumed by well-off women in the privacy of their homes. In the eighteenth century it was vigorously but not altogether successfully promoted by the East India Company, but when import duties on tea were abolished around 1840 it came down rapidly in price and began to spread in popularity across a wide spectrum of society. It was available in growing numbers of coffee houses and added another element to the decline of these institutions. Tea-drinking never had the wide-ranging impact of coffee house culture.

In his *Curiosities of Literature* (1817) an astute observer, Isaac D'Israeli, the father of future prime minister Benjamin Disraeli, wrote about the visible decline in the popularity of coffee houses:

> The frequenting of coffee houses is a custom which has declined within our recollection, since institutions of a higher character, and society itself, has so much improved within late years. They were, however, the common assemblies of all classes of society. The

mercantile man, the man of letters, and the man of fashion, had their appropriate coffee houses.

Although there were still probably as many as 1,400 coffee houses in the London area at the end of the nineteenth century, the days in which they played a major role in commerce and significantly influenced the manners, morals and the politics of the nation were most certainly over. However, some had changed the nature of their business and were offering other services, such as accommodation. The London Coffee House on Ludgate Hill was described in a London directory of 1793 as 'a large and superb mansion with a profusion of attendants, the first rate cooks, the best waiters, the smartest chambermaids, hair dressers, porters and shoe-blacks'. This is a long way from the original concept of the coffee house.

As coffee house culture went into terminal decline, the coffee houses themselves were succeeded by more egalitarian and humble institutions known as coffee rooms, which were again largely patronised by men. The initiative for many of these came from the temperance movement, which formed a very powerful lobby in Victorian society. The virtues of coffee were contrasted with the vices of alcohol and efforts were made to lure working men away from the tavern, the beer house and what was euphemistically called the public house.

The arrival on the scene of coffee rooms coincided with a fall in the price of coffee. Coffee, well laced with sugar, was promoted as providing a nutritious and sustaining start to the day for the workman or office worker who previously might well have had a pint or two of beer before getting to his place of employment. The coffee rooms were open from early in the morning until late in the evening and food was available as well as newspapers and journals. Furnishings and fittings were not unlike those to be found in pubs. In 1838 London had 332 coffee rooms. By 1843 there were possibly as many as 1,800. Charles Dickens visited coffee rooms, usually having half a pint of coffee and a slice of bread and butter. He mentions them in his writings and makes it clear that while there were some quite superior establishments, others were dirty and ill-smelling. However, G. Dodd's *The Food of London* published in 1856 lavished praise on coffee shops: 'The good fire, the bright light, the supply of newspapers and magazines, and the cup of simple beverage, are obtainable for a few pence; and there can be little question that these places conduce to sobriety and general intelligence.'

In the competition for the pennies and the leisure time of the working man, the pubs and other drinking places were still winning, much to the chagrin of the temperance lobby. The latter then hit on the idea of providing establishments with the same kind of entertainment and surroundings – and even the conviviality of the public house, they hoped – but where coffee, soft drinks and other similar refreshments were available rather than the 'demon drink'. Food would also be available, a service lacking in most Victorian drinking places. Probably the first of these 'coffee taverns' was opened in Dundee in 1853, although it was not until 1873 that such an establishment was opened in London. This was the Edinburgh Castle Coffee Palace, converted from a previously notorious gin palace and located in Limehouse, close to the Pool of London. A chain of 'British Workman Public Houses' was established by the National Temperance League, while the People's Café Company opened a number of premises, usually near places where large numbers of working people were employed, as did the Coffee Tavern Company Limited.

Many of these places looked like pubs, inside and out, and indeed in many cases had been converted from them. They sported bars for those addicted to 'vertical drinking' and often had the mirrors, etched glass windows and general air of opulence of many of the gin palaces themselves. Plenty of seating was available and there were frequently reading rooms and games rooms. Some had sleeping accommodation. They even had 'jug and bottle' departments for those who wished to consume their beverages off the premises.

They had everything except the alcohol. To compensate, some sold Cox's Anti-Burton, which, described as a perfect substitute for mild ale, was promoted in ringing terms as 'Awarded First Prize by Ely Diocesan Branch of the Church of England Temperance Society'. What greater endorsement could there be?

Although in 1879 London possessed around 100 of these pubs without beer, not surprisingly, the bulk of working men continued to patronise the public houses. The leaders of the temperance movement were often wealthy upper-class High Church Tories who treated drink and the problems associated with it as if they were the cause of social distress rather than a symptom of the despair created by a deeply flawed social and economic system. They tended to adopt an extremely patronising attitude towards the people they purported to be helping. Naturally this was resented, and the establishments serving coffee and other non-alcoholic drinks never seriously threatened the profits of the brewers and distillers. 'The cup which cheers but does not inebriate' never caught on to the extent that its temperance promoters had hoped.

Coffee was among the various drinks served in London's many pleasure gardens. These enjoyed a brief vogue with the rich and fashionable before the latter took themselves off in search of fresh delights elsewhere, whereupon the pleasure garden usually went into freefall, ending up as little more than a place where the local *demi-mondes* and rakehells came together for mutual enjoyment. The owners went broke and the pleasure gardens closed. Tea gardens did not necessarily do much better. Other competition for the coffee houses came from the hotels, cafés and chains of restaurants that opened in significant numbers in London in the second half of the nineteenth century.

For a nation perceived as a hotbed of incurable and almost insatiable tea-drinkers, it may come as a surprise that so much coffee was consumed during the heyday of the coffee house. That tea won is perhaps because it was much quicker and simpler to prepare than coffee. Basically all that was needed was tea and the equipment for boiling water. It did not help the cause of coffee that there were a number of revelations about the impurities and adulterants contained in almost all brands of coffee. One investigator in 1848 showed that a substance analysed as baked horse's liver was added to some brands. The consumption of coffee consequently fell by over 40 per cent between 1852 and 1890, while tea consumption rose spectacularly during the same period.

Scarcely had traditional coffee houses largely disappeared from the scene than they began to feature in dewy-eyed nostalgia for the good old days. A correspondent calling himself Harry Honeycombe, writing in the *New Monthly Magazine* in 1826, remarked, 'I never pass Covent Garden . . . without thinking of all the old coffee houses and the wits, so I can never reflect, without impatience, that there are no such meetings now, and no coffee room that looks as if it would suit them.' In his magisterial *History of England* completed in 1855, Lord Macaulay argued that the coffee house had played a vital role in the development of democracy, being a very important medium through which public opinion in London, and by implication throughout the nation, was developed and channelled.

CHAPTER 8

The Social and Economic Impact of the Coffee Houses

Coffee arrives, that grave and wholesome liquor
That heals the stomach, makes the genius quicker,
Relives the memory, revives the sad,
And cheers the spirits without making mad . . .

Coffee houses played a vital role in the development of what historians have characterised as the 'public sphere'. They were one among a number of social institutions including taverns, clubs, journals, newspapers and periodicals which allowed people of the time to meet either in person or via the printed word and to create, give voice to, exchange and take in new ideas, opinions and perspectives. In so doing they created the notion of 'public opinion' or the 'public sphere'. This somewhat amorphous but important concept involved the forming of a corpus of views which had an increasingly significant influence in politics, public affairs, the arts, the sciences and elsewhere. As *The Craftsman* of 20 March 1727 said: 'I could wish that you would now and then, of an evening, come incognito to the public coffee houses . . . for then you will be truly informed of the opinions and sentiments of mankind.' In today's terms this activity could perhaps be called cultural networking.

The Enlightenment is a term used to describe a range of new cultural and intellectual attitudes and practices that emerged in Western Europe in the eighteenth century. A complex concept, it is perhaps most easily characterised as embracing a critical scrutinising of existing practices and beliefs and the exploration of new intellectual possibilities, especially through the use of reason and, where applicable, observation and experimentation. A feature was anti-clericalism and the assertion of the right of laymen to pronounce on those matters of morality and metaphysics which the Church had traditionally tried to monopolise. Whereas the Church's emphasis was that this life was a preparation for the hereafter, Enlightenment thinkers emphasised that the task was to work towards improving this life.

Coffee houses encouraged rational, critical and informed discussion among their patrons. In theory what the speaker had to say was more important than who he was, but it would be misleading to see this as a particularly democratic aspect of coffee house culture. The coffee houses were class institutions within a very hierarchical society. Most patrons can be loosely described as middle class, while others were attracted to the coffee house for the purposes of commerce or for their interest in ideas in the broadest sense. By definition this excluded not only many other middle-class people but also the vast bulk of the working classes whose interminable struggle to eke out a living left them with little time or inclination for the pursuit of ideas for their own sake.

The surviving letters, journals and biographies of mid- and late eighteenth-century people indicate that this was a period of remarkable sociability. This is of course a sweeping generalisation, but it was a time when more and more people lived in and used towns, and many of these people were leisured. Any reader, for example, of Boswell's *Life of Johnson* will notice how much of the life of the London literati was spent in social groups and engaged in discussion of at least a fairly serious kind. There was a thirst for intellectual stimulation. In some towns and cities the focus was the Literary and Philosophical Society or its equivalent. In London the role was played for at least a hundred years by the coffee houses. At their best, those taking part could bring to the discussion a remarkable range of knowledge and experience. At Slaughter's in the 1760s a get-together included the amateur inventor Richard Lovell Edgeworth, the surgeon John Hunter, the sailor-geographer Captain James Cook, the Swedish botanist Daniel Charles Solander and the civil engineer John Smeaton.

Those who patronised coffee houses were predominantly male, so any attempt to give the coffee houses a prominent place in the history of emerging democratic tendencies in Britain has to be tempered by the fact that they welcomed few women customers. Contemporary observations make it clear that women worked as servants in coffee houses and there were also women, wives or widows of male proprietors, who presided over proceedings and, in the case of widows, sometimes took over the ownership. Some of them, by virtue of their position, carved out quite influential roles for themselves, disseminating the latest news and gossip and also perhaps enjoying the role of confidantes to their customers. Where these customers were the great and good, this could indeed have given the women a powerful position. Those who were really successful must have been able to employ considerable tact and discretion.

Nothing spreads more quickly than rumour and so-called secrets, especially if they are of a scandalous or salacious nature. The coffee houses were the medium through which information or sometimes misinformation developed and was disseminated. Everyone likes to feel that they are in possession of privy information: being first with the news confers a sense of power. Inevitably, rumours, stories and titbits of information became enlarged and exaggerated as they were told and retold, the tongue moving faster than the feet – and often faster than the brain.

It was from within coffee houses that the journalists of the day garnered much of their material. The contents of early periodicals such as the *Tatler* and the *Spectator* sometimes consisted of little more than the news and gossip currently coursing around the coffee houses. Not everyone took the tittle-tattle too seriously. In 'A Tale of a Tub' (1704) Jonathan Swift wrote about MPs who were silent during proceedings in the House of Commons but 'were loud in the Coffee house, where they nightly adjourn to chew the Cud of Politicks, and are encompass'd with a Ring of Disciples who lye in wait to catch up their Droppings'.

Another observer, Tom Brown, pithily captured the many-sided but sometimes lightweight nature of the discussions when he noted in 1700 that 'some were discoursing of all sorts of Government, Monarchical, Aristocratical, and Democratical; some about the choice of mayors, sheriffs and aldermen; and others of the transcendent virtues of vinegar, pepper and mustard'.

Dealing only with information that is totally verifiable has never been regarded as a priority by those professing to be journalists. Joseph Addison was another who had the measure of coffee house talk. One day he visited a number of coffee houses in the course of an experiment in monitoring the progress of a rumour, totally without foundation, that the King of France had died. His first call was at the St James coffee house where he found

the whole outward room in a buzz of Politics. The speculations were but very indifferent towards the door but grew finer as you advanced to the upper end of the room, and were so very much improved by a Knot of theorists, who sat in the inner room, within the steams of the coffee pot, that I there heard the whole Spanish monarchy disposed of, and all the line of Bourbon provided for in less than a quarter of an hour. (The *Spectator*, 12 June 1712.)

Addison's understanding of the nature of Chinese whispers developed by leaps and bounds as he made his way from one coffee house to another, hearing slightly different versions of the same basic story. In every case it was evident that none of those eagerly holding forth on the significance of the French King's death had bothered to verify whether the death had actually occurred. In Will's, he heard a group of patrons engaged in an earnest discussion about the shortage of French poets of sufficient gravity to do justice to an elegy for the dead monarch.

In spite of the shallowness and often fallacious nature of the information on which the discussions were based, coffee houses and their culture played a key role in fostering a growing sense of scepticism towards a whole range of long-held popular beliefs and practices. A sense of rational, dispassionate criticism was applied to the examination of such things as witchcraft and superstition and also many religious assumptions. This led to coffee houses being branded by some as atheist institutions. In fact, scoffing, debunking and the holding up to ridicule of all manner of institutions and of those individuals who were pompous or who took themselves too seriously, were very much the forte of many coffee house devotees. Such attitudes did not accord with the ideal of politeness and respect for one's fellows and their views and opinions.

Coffee houses were an important factor in the development of clubs and societies. One of the earliest clubs to meet regularly at a coffee house was the Rota, established in 1659 at the Turk's Head coffee house in Westminster. This was a political club, but it was followed by many devoted to a variety of artistic and scientific interests. The Royal Society, or, to give its full name, the Royal Society for the Promotion of Natural Knowledge, was founded in 1660 and received a royal charter in 1662. This august body spawned numerous specialist offshoots that met in the many coffee houses to be found around the Strand and Fleet Street. What went on to become the Royal Society of Arts, for example, was established in

1754 in Rawthmell's Coffee House in Covent Garden. Coffee houses provided a venue for many early lodges of the freemasonry movement, which traces its modern history back to the first quarter of the eighteenth century.

The profession of coffee house keeper was a new one, akin to but distinct and different from that of tavern-, alehouse- or inn-keeper. The trade was not without its risks. Coffee was sold at a penny a dish or portion, but the wholesale price might fluctuate widely because of factors totally out of the proprietor's control. This put pressure on profit margins, and so there was always a temptation for the coffee house proprietor to buy the commodity on which his livelihood depended in an adulterated or otherwise debased form. Such pernicious practices were not always easy to detect but could damage the health of those drinking such products. The issue of safeguarding the consumer through methods of inspection, prevention and, if necessary, prosecution, are seen as essential aspects of public health policy in modern society. In Britain the initial fight to establish such agencies took place in the nineteenth century. A casual skimming of the news reveals that the issue is as pertinent today as it was in the age of the coffee house.

In the early days of the coffee houses the beverage was served in dishes or small bowls, the shape of which helped to cool the liquid more quickly. The growing consumption of hot drinks such as coffee and tea provided a considerable stimulus to the English pottery industry, but simultaneously reduced the demand for drinking vessels made of pewter. In 1740 the English pottery industry began to produce cups specially designed for coffee-drinking and in the 1760s they developed a creamware with a delicate, even translucent appearance that was able to resist the heat of boiling liquid. Specialised pots for the serving of coffee were also developed, and these were usually made of copper and were often octagonal in shape. A shop in Aldgate in the City of London made a speciality of stocking 'coffee accessories'. These included sugar dishes, tea, chocolate and coffee cups and saucers and a range of pots.

In helping to kick-start the development of the English pottery industry, the coffee houses unwittingly contributed to the extraordinary conjuncture of factors that together made up the Industrial Revolution, part of the process whereby Britain changed from a pre-dominantly rural and agriculturally based society into one characterised by its urban and industrial nature. The importance to Britain and the world of this process was incalculable. Specifically, the demand for pottery and ceramics, especially from Staffordshire, required their manufacturers to find a better means of bringing in coal for fuel and the china clay they needed as a raw material, and transporting their fragile finished products to the markets. For several decades it was the canals that performed that service, with considerable success.

The coffee houses represent an important step in the development of two interlinking features of modern society, the emergence as a major economic factor of both the hospitality and leisure industries. The amazing rise in the popularity of coffee-drinking as well as tea, cocoa and chocolate was early evidence of the shrinking of the globe and of the production of primary cash crops in what are now called developing countries for export to the advanced countries to meet the demand for luxury items. Producer and consumer became bonded together in an international trading relationship which, then as now, only served to emphasise the gulf between the richer and the poorer nations of the world.

Further Reading

Burke, T., *English Night Life*, London, 1941

——, *The English Townsman*, London, 1946

Clayton, A., *London's Coffee Houses: A Stimulating Story*, London, 2003

Ehrman, E. and Forsyth, H. *et al.*, *London Eats Out: 500 Years of Capital Dining*, London, 1999

Ellis, A., *The Penny Universities. A History of the Coffee Houses*, London, 1956

Ellis, M., *The Coffee House. A Cultural History*, London, 2004

Flower, R. and Jones, M.W., *Lloyd's of London, An Illustrated History*, London, 1974

Latham, J., *The Pleasure of Your Company. A History of Manners and Meals*, London, 1972

Lillywhite, B., *London Coffee Houses*, London, 1963

Tames, R., *Feeding London: A Taste of History*, London, 2003